MW01122434

When the World
Is Not Our Home

ALSO BY SUSAN MUSGRAVE

FICTION

The Charcoal Burners (1980)
The Dancing Chicken (1990)
Cargo of Orchids (2000)

POETRY

Songs of the Sea-Witch (1970)
Entrance of the Celebrant (1972)
Grave-Dirt and Selected Strawberries (1973)
The Impstone (1976)
Kiskatinaw Songs (with Seán Virgo, 1978)
Selected Strawberries and Other Poems (1977)
Becky Swan's Book (1977)
A Man to Marry, A Man to Bury (1979)
Tarts and Muggers:Poems New and Selected (1982)
Cocktails at the Mausoleum (1985)
The Embalmer's Art: Poems New and Selected (1991)
Forcing the Narcissus (1994)
Things That Keep and Do Not Change (1999)
What the Small Day Cannot Hold: Collected Poems 1970-1985
Obituary of Light: the Sangan River Meditations (2009)

CHILDREN'S

Gullband (1973)
Hag head (1980)
Kestrel and Leonardo (1990)
Dreams are More Real than Bathtubs (1999)

NONFICTION

Great Musgrave (1988)
Musgrave Landing: Musings on the Writing Life (1991)
You're in Canada Now . . . A Memoir of Sorts (2005)

When the World
Is Not Our Home

Selected Poems
1985-2000

Susan Musgrave

thistledown press

Thistledown Press Ltd.
633 Main Street
Saskatoon, Saskatchewan, S7H 0J8
www.thistledownpress.com

Library and Archives Canada Cataloguing in Publication
Musgrave, Susan, 1951-
[Poems. Selections]
When the world is not our home : selected poems, 1985-2000 / Susan Musgrave.

ISBN 978-1-897235-67-6
I. Title. II. Title: Poems. Selections.
PS8576.U7A6 2009   C811'.54   C2009-904217-7

Cover photograph: ©ilja herb/Aurora
Cover and book design by Jackie Forrie
Printed and bound in Canada

Mixed Sources
Cert no. SW-COC-001271
© 1996 FSC
FSC

Thistledown Press gratefully acknowledges the financial assistance of the Canada Council for the Arts, the Saskatchewan Arts Board, and the Government of Canada through the Book Publishing Industry Development Program for its publishing program.

 Canada Council   Conseil des Arts
for the Arts   du Canada
 SASKATCHEWAN
ARTS BOARD
 Canadian   Patrimoine
Heritage   canadien

ACKNOWLEDGEMENTS

The poems in this book have been selected from my two precious collections, *Forcing the Narcissus* (McClelland & Stewart, 1994) and *Things That Keep and do Not Change* (McClelland & Stewart, 1999).

A number of these poems were published by Reference West in a chapbook entitled *In the Small Hours of the Rain*, which won the b.p. nichol Poetry Chapbook Award.

The Spiritualization of Cruelty, a portfolio including six of my poems and drawings by Pavel Skalnik, was published as a limited, lettered and numbered edition by Lake Gallery of Toronto.

Thanks to Marilyn Bowering for the echo of her line, "love jumps away . . . " and to Robert Penn Warren, to whom the last line of "Forcing the Narcissus" owes a debt. The line "things that keep and do not change" is from the poem "Silver Lake" by Brigit Pegeen Kelly, reprinted by permission of BOA Editions in New York.

The lines in italics in "Becoming: *Essay on Man*" are from Alexander Pope's "Essay on Man". The poem referred to, "A Violation", is by Richard Jackson.

The poem titles in the sequence "The Selected poems of Paul Durcan" were inspired by the chapter headings in *Louisiana Power and Light*, a novel by John Dufresne.

A number of these poems, under the title "The Gold Luck of Carp" won the CBC/Tilden Award for Poetry and were broadcast on the CBC.

Contents

"There are places where the heart cannot rest,
where the best you can do is be at home with the rootless."
— Unknown

WATER TREMBLING AT THE RIM
The Process of Revision

Paul Valéry, of "poems are never finished they are only abandoned" fame, wrote that a work is never completed except by some accident such as weariness, satisfaction, the need to deliver, or death. The accident of satisfaction is one I have mostly escaped, though not so weariness and the need to deliver. As far as completion goes, death's still waiting to finalize my brief biography: Susan Musgrave, 1951 –

The poems that make up this book — selected from my two previous collections, *Forcing the Narcissus* (M&S, 1994) and *Things That Keep But Do Not Change* (1999) are those I feel have abandoned me, but insist we keep in touch. Poems abandon us when they're ready to enter what we refer to as the public realm, unencumbered by the presence of their creators. (There is no higher compliment, in my mind, than to find a line from one of my poems pencilled on a bathroom wall, attributed to "Unknown" or "Anonymous" — it's humbling but satisfyingly private, like Bob Dylan's desire to be buried in an unmarked grave.)

But how do we know when it's time to let a poem go? Jane Hirshfield says that what is required is no less than our "alert responsiveness" to the poem's effects, that we must give not only our rapt attention but our whole presence "to each shift in the currents of language with an answering shift in our own being."

"Poems," she writes, "despite the way they are sometimes taught, are not crossword-puzzle constructions; first drafts, and many stages of revision, take place at a level closer to daydream. But daydream with an added intensity; while writing, the mind moves between consciousness and the unconscious in the effortless effort of concentration. The result, if the poet's intensity of attention is sufficient, will be a poem that brims with its own knowledge, water trembling as if miraculously above the edge of a cup."

There is no statute of limitations when it comes to revising poetry. It isn't unusual for poets to continue working on a poem even after it appears in print. Donald Hall in the interview, "Flying Revision's Flag," (from *Kestril*, 1993 reprinted on the Poets.org website http://www.poets.org/viewmedia.php/prmMID/16223) explains how he goes about the process of revision. "At first the poem is volatile and changeable in the extreme; from time to time it slows down and stops. When it stops and will not move again, I show it to Jane (the poet Jane Kenyon, who died of leukemia in 1995) and to other friends, and either they tell me to leave it alone, or they show me errors, which I change . . . I finish the poem, with the help of my friends, publish it, it comes out in a magazine — and when the magazine arrives in the mail I tinker with the poem some more."

With the help of my friends, and editors, the poems in this selection have shifted, and shape-shifted through my long days' daydreaming into night. "Cut these words and they would bleed," Ralph Waldo Emerson wrote, of Montaigne's unassailable essays, and while I like to think that my poems will never need anything as serious as a heart transplant or a lobotomy, most of them have survived invasive surgery of some sort — everything from bypasses to stitches. Once, when appointed the kind of editor for whom no passion in the world equalled his passion to alter someone else's draft, I discovered how terribly carefully I had chosen every word in each poem I wrote, including (and sometimes especially) the words "and", "if" and "but" — that I knew what I was doing more than I trusted that I knew what I was doing. This editor for example, suggested I change a line in "The Gift": "she feels her reaching to stitch it up/the sad equipment of womanhood" to "she feels her reaching to stitch up the sad equipment of womanhood."

Two things happen when you cut that small word "it". One is you lose the moment's hesitation, the moment that allows the reader to wonder, "what is 'it'"? Secondly, you lose a rhyme with "stitch". Cut this word, and "it" would bleed. (Cutting "it" in this instance would be like taking William Matthews' line, which I use as a title, "Here It Comes, Grief's Beautiful Blow-Job" and shortening it to "Here Comes Grief's Beautiful Blow-Job".)

Seán Virgo warned me that a line in "One Evening, the Wind Rising, It began . . . " verged on the sentimental: "Tears fell like spring rain down her face . . . " but I left it as is. I remember reading that the best art approaches the edge of sentimentality (I have resisted using "verges on sentimentality" because — why must sentimentality always "verge"?) but resists falling over it. This may be the one occasion when I have not taken Seán's spot-on editorial advice. He has that annoying and uncanny sense of being able to pick out the one word, the one line, you have been trying to let yourself get away with, the not-quite-right line you trick yourself into believing nobody else will see.

Astrid Egger, from Queen Charlotte City, wrote me a letter after attending a reading I gave at the Victoria School of Writing. I'd read "The Laughter in the Kitchen," and Astrid took exception to my used of the word "vagina".

> " . . . . We can
> build a new house when I make lots of good
> money," my daughter says, butting out
> the Popeye candy cigarette she won
> from the neighbour boy for showing him
> her vagina through a slit in the split
> cedar fence. I wept, told her next time,
>
> baby, hold out for a whole pack,
> trying to be brave, the way only a mother
> could."

Astrid maintained that my daughter would have needed a speculum in order for the neighbour boy to view her vagina, that women, after all this time, still do not know the names of their private parts, and the word I should have used was "vulva". I tried this out on my friend Lorna Crozier, and Lorna said, no, "vagina" was generic, the way we say "mouth" as a general area, meaning everything — lips, tongue, teeth and canker sores. She taught my poem the following year at UVic and gave the students a list of possible alternates for "vagina": cunt, pussy, vulva, labia minora, and so on. The consensus was that "vagina" fit, that it was perhaps not anatomically correct, but was the best word for the poem, given that the word is probably what a child would have used. (No doubt Astrid would say, rightly so I see now, that I have taught my daughter the wrong name for her body part. I have since read that the whole area is actually called the clitoris, so now I am more confused than before Astrid even began our vagina dialogue.)

But back to the subject of tinkering: there have been times when I've gone on fine-tuning a poem even after it has been carved in stone, or at least printed on acid-free paper in a book. In the poem that became the title of my collection *Forcing the Narcissus*, I use an image of feeling the wind through "my rice paper door" but I didn't even know this wasn't the image I'd been looking for until I was walking down Roncesvalle in Toronto, in the winter of 1995, a year after the book had been released. I saw a sign in a florist's window — "Paper-whites for sale," and realized at once it was "paper-white" I hadn't known I hadn't been looking for (I still picture my grandmother forcing her paper-white narcissus every Christmas when I was a child). "Rice paper" had to go. In this book, at last, I can make it right.

What I learned from this experience is that even though you think a poem has abandoned you, the subconscious may still be hanging on to it, and that mental knots often loosen spontaneously when you step away from the task. I have also learned that the poem, in and of itself, has something to say about the final form it is determined to take, despite whatever the writer intended. You must be attuned to the poem's effects, alert to the expectations raised by any new word you decide to substitute for another, and doubly aware of how the poem changes those expectations in order to satisfy itself. Rewriting, then, is not just a matter of craft and technique, but a whole new way of seeing, a re-vision.

All the poems in this book were written in the 80s and 90s, which is not so long ago that I am incapable of re-entering the worlds within the words. Galway Kinnell, in the introduction to his *Three Books*, says revision is most likely to fail if many years have passed between the reflective phase of the creation and the impulse to rewrite. He calls it the Law of Elapsed Time.

The majority of the (mostly very small) changes I have made are not, in fact, re-visions or re-imaginings, they are more along the lines of a belated attempt, not to perfect the poems (perfection in the root sense of the word, "thoroughly done") but to carry them a degree further towards that point where I can, for better or worse, let them go. Sometimes the change can be as small as one letter, an "a" into an "an," for example. (What a difference a single letter can make. I had a hologram on my Toy Car http://www.flickr.com/photos/yewco/237661124/ that read, "I was a deprived child" if you looked at it one way, and "I was a depraved child" if you turned your head slightly, and looked at it from a different angle.) My experience with trying to rewrite old material is that it can easily end up making the poem worse. "When you substitute what seems like a splendid new passage for an old awkward one, in a poem that has been apparently finished for years, it may seem that you have lifted it at last out of mediocrity, but when you look in on it the next day, you may find it lying in ruins," Galway Kinnell says. "That is because there is a poetic equivalent to the organ transplant rejection syndrome. The new passage often won't cohere with the rest — in mood, in language, even in intent — and for better or worse the poem must make do with the original lines." For this reason I rarely try — once time has elapsed — to rewrite whole stanzas, unless I am convinced the revisions will "take".

Here are some examples of the small changes I did make. In "The Long Way Home":

"I did not know I was living my life then
for what I have become now"

became

"I did not know I was living my life then
for what I have become"

In "Razor Wire, Millhaven Penitentiary":
" . . . In so much blackness
the heart leaps, jumps a beat
by the wall, and then
goes over."

became

" . . . In so much blackness
the heart leaps, jumps a beat
by the wall, goes over."

Again I'd wanted a moment's hesitation before going over the wall, which, I believed, the words "and then" provided. Ultimately I changed it, though, and looking at it today, I still think I did the right thing by this poem.

Usually, though, by the time I feel a poem is ready to abandon me (i.e. to be included in a book, which brings to mind Truman Capote's view of finishing a book — "it's like you took a child out in the yard and shot it") it has been through numerous revisions already; "Depression in Debrecen" underwent ninety-six rewrites — substantial rewrites, not just those where I changed one word, or two. Most of my poems go through a minimum of twenty drafts; there's only one that ever "came out" whole. I wrote it, in my head, on a walk, committed it to memory, got home, typed it out, and never changed a word of it. It was ("Conversation During the Omelette Aux Fines Herbes" published by Beach Holme Press in *What the Small Day Cannot Hold: Collected Poems 1970-1985*) unlike any poem I'd ever written (or have written since) and is still the only one of my poems I can recite by heart. I wish more poems would take possession of me this way.

Something else I have taken to rewriting is other writers' lines. Permissions to quote snatches of poetry or songs, in epigraphs or as lines within the text of poems, has become, in many cases, unaffordable, and this I think is a shame. We all suffer as a result because we risk not being exposed to the works of poets we might otherwise never hear of. After I wrote "Poison" I requested what seemed to me fair use of a Joni Mitchell line, about looking at life from two different sides, but couldn't afford the fee her people demanded, which was twice the amount of my advance. I re-visioned her line as this:

> " . . . No one spoke
> of choice as I sat cramped in the back
> of the Buick with my mother sighing
> how she'd looked at life from both sides
> of the same two bits, and my father
> threatening to drive the car off
> the biggest bluff if she didn't quit."

. . . and was pleased with my ability to improve upon Joni Mitchell's line (if I do say so myself) at the same time managing to side-step copyright law. It is usually up to the individual writer to grant permission for his or her work to be quoted, and most writers are pleased to have their lines acknowledged. There are exceptions — Mary Oliver wouldn't let Lorna Crozier use one of her lines as an epigraph, and gave no reason why — but most of us are happy to spread the serendipity. I don't know how many times I've read from my series, "The Selected Poems of Paul Durcan" and had members of the audience ask where can they buy his books! But I love Paul's work and don't begrudge him, for a moment, the fame he has received as a result of my poems singing his praise. (It would be nice if he coughed up a percentage of his royalties, but I understand it if he's lost the transit number to my numbered Swiss bank account.)

One place Galway Kinnell's Law of Elapsed Time applies, especially, is in relation to line breaks. Take old poems and try and teach them new line breaks at your own peril! I changed only one break in this book, and that was in "Something Has to Give in a Life". The poem as it appeared in *Things That Keep and Do Not Change*, ended:

> "We woke the baby with our singing
> and crying. Her heartbeat was something
> always to be remembered,
> something to love forever."

and now the last two lines read:

> "We woke the baby with our singing
> and crying. Her heartbeat was something
> always to be remembered, something
> to love forever."

I may live to regret this change, but I can always re-revise back to a previous draft in a subsequent edition, if the poem insists.

Susan Musgrave
Haida Gwaii, May, 2009

When the World
Is Not Our Home

and bread by the woodstove
waiting to be punched down again.
I step out into the dark
morning, find the last white flowers
in a Mason jar by the door
and a note from a friend saying
he would call again later. I go back
into the kitchen, tomatoes
on the windowsill after rain,
small things but vast
if you desire them.

The deep fresh red.
This life rushing towards me.

SOMETHING HAS TO GIVE IN A LIFE

Last night I took a gun
and fired it at something, maybe you
Afterwards, after the silence,
there was a hole as big as my heart
and the light shone through.

I keep trying to believe in pain
because pain, like love,
so easily mystified, holds true.

We woke the baby with our singing
and crying. Her heartbeat was something
always to be remembered, something
to love forever.

raining. I peeked out from behind the blinds
while the lights blinked and my mother went
from room to room in her silence, lighting
the few candles. Flowers on their drunken stems
were opening themselves like brides, and I tried
to explain to my daughter how she couldn't go out
and play any longer in that garden.

Tears fell like spring rain down her face
when I said I thought death might be something
we could return from as another life.
She didn't want to hear this and pushed me
away. She said she wanted to be herself,
always. She wanted me, too, to be who I am.

I have reached an age when even a spring
rain falling on spring ground can make me
less of what I am. So I told her then what I've tried
to believe in my life, that we don't have to die,
ever. Victorious she turned to me, like the flowers
of this world, the brilliance sliding from her.

THE MOMENT

The legless man in the motel room next to me
listens to Country and Western music
all night, an endless song
about going down on his knees
for some faithless woman's love.
I turn in my bed, thinking of you
the day we thought our daughter
had gone missing. The moment before
she disappeared you'd seen a stranger
on the block, the kind who wore
a stained suit from the Sally Ann, the kind
who couldn't know innocence
existed. Our daughter was supposed to be

next door, playing in the fenced yard
with two neighbour boys. You'd been
on the phone and I'd turned my back
on the moment to do something
predictable — move the garden sprinkler,
open the morning mail — acts
that would never again seem so ordinary
once we'd made up our minds
between burial or cremation. Your body

had never felt so alive as you took off
in the car, driving down
every back lane, listening for her
glove-muffled cries. You drove

deeper and deeper into the kind of hell
we reserve for ourselves and never want
our children to have to know. You knew

at this moment she could only be suffering
in the hands of that stranger who would afterwards
stuff her trusting body into a single forest
green Glad Bag, then tote her to the park.

They would find her legs first, dangling
from the swing, shoes on the wrong feet
as usual, arms hanging from the jungle
gym. I'd want to touch, to straighten
her turned-in toes: how clumsily
we lived on this earth!

She was lost only for a moment, locked
in a spare bedroom with the two boys
next door, not wanting her privacy interrupted,
but in that moment when she was gone
forever, death in all his beautiful variety
sang to us, off-key and aching
inside our cheated hearts.

THE LAUGHTER IN THE KITCHEN

All day our daughter and her best friend
have been playing marriage, destroying
the house to make it the way they need it
to be. They've shoved the loveseat
across the bedroom door to form a barricade,
overturned the armchairs to give themselves
temporary shelters. They've even rolled
the carpet back, "so the carpet won't get
beer spilled on it," my daughter, pretending
to be Dad, explains, when I complain:
the house doesn't feel like my own anymore
but still I have to live in it. "We can

build a new house when I make lots of good
money," my daughter says, butting out
the Popeye candy cigarette she won
from the neighbour boy for showing him
her vagina through a slit in the split
cedar fence. I wept, told her next time,

baby, hold out for a whole pack,
trying to be brave, the way only a mother
could. "We can't build anything if you
keep drinking drugs," the tiny wife bursts
as my daughter keels into the cookstove
and pretends to catch fire, the laughter
in the kitchen filling the house
where we tried to live. What has become

of my young life, the man who once pressed
a fistful of crocuses between my breasts
and made love to me on the kitchen floor
while beyond, on the river,
a loudspeaker-toting paddleboat carried

honeymooners to the mouth. Later we took
the same cruise, pretending to be newlyweds
ourselves, holding hands on the tipping deck
with others who took photographs to prove
they had truly been there, they had
loved each other — once. The laughter

in the kitchen reminds me: grief
is a burden, something to be shaken
like the foxgloves in our garden, stooping
under the weight of their seeds. I've learned
the lessons of pain, now wait for the same
light that makes my daughter's face so
luminous and wise as she says to her small friend,
"Now you be Dad. You've got no body so you can't
get away. I'll be the mother this time."

WHERE HE LIVES

In the room where you sleep you take the postcard
your father sent from the country where he lives
and hold it under your night-light as if
light could bring him closer and be his awakening.

What can I tell you? What you see is true,
a woman wades naked into the sea and to you
she looks beautiful, to you it seems
natural. The waves make no sound breaking up
on the shore and you are not to know this
naked beautiful woman is sad and usual underneath.

I turn out your light because we dream
deeper in darkness, and mourn you all night as if
suddenly you are not there any more, as if
you have been left with no one.

The Noise a Skeleton Makes
Trying on a New Body

At night in the hospital, far
from the dark shore your body washed
up on, I hear water lapping
under a becalmed hull, your lungs still
gulping air, then releasing it. Grief
is a voyeur here, peeping from the nest
of wild birds outside the barred window
in the pear tree that will never bear,
at least not this time around.
I stroke your thin hands, kiss
the track marks along your arms,
the veins that took me somewhere
I never intended to go. At first

the sound is indistinguishable
from the rest, the noise your body makes
trying to laugh, feel, sit up in bed
as our daughter arranges cream-coloured
freesias in the blue vase beside your head
and John, the Irishman, lights
a contraband cigarette. At first
I am resigned, I have been getting used
to the future. But then I begin to believe
you'll do it, this time you'll get better
forever again, one day

we might even be able to talk
without raising our voices. What
would we hear each other say
as our daughter turns the flowers so they
too, can get a good view of the room
and what lies beyond? Our daughter

who looks like you. She says she can
smell and taste and hear everything,
especially your sadness. Sometimes
your sadness hurts her ears. To show you how
how much, she puts her hands over her ears
then lays her trembling fingers on your face
as if they can still give you the power
to heal. Now your hands flail towards her
grace like birds first entering the sky
they've so often failed to reach.

HISTORY LESSON

The child is dancing. It's all
she can do now that her mother lies
face down in the weeds and her father's
teeth have been broken like the small-paned
windows in the home they'd made together
on the outskirts of a town. Her parents

were ordinary people tending their garden
when the terrorists arrived. How lush
that garden might have become
if it hadn't been for desire!

The man watching from the balcony next door
takes an historical overview.
He believe terrorism is the rage
of the literati in its last stage.
He's seen so many people exterminated
he's beginning to feel experienced.

The child stares up at the man.
To her he has always been ordinary
too — someone to be avoided, maybe
even feared. But now his interest
in her makes her nipples grow hard
and she's able to see her distant
former life as it could have been,
without pain, and it makes her feel
the rage of every grown-up woman.

She cuts new lips from her mother's
face and paints some lipstick on.
She makes a smile from her father's
teeth and puts it in on, and history
moves on, too, in the rear view
mirror of the car she's driving

away into the future. There's one more dead
body in the trunk of the car, whose
it is she doesn't know yet.

The man sees through all these
stages. It's any suburban street
on any weekday morning, and the school bus
has yet to arrive. Maybe there's no school
today, no lessons.

The man has seen history repeated
and still he'd like to see more.
He wants there to be much more than just
his ex-wife driving into the future
with their only child in the trunk of the car,
the child, who, moments ago, tried dancing.

My Girl Is Entering the First Grade

We're late, the car has engine problems
and the temperature outside is
falling. My daughter wants to know
how life begins. I pump the gas, hoping
for another miracle.

Our grown cats loll on the lawn, some
innocent pink thing between them
giving its final whimper. I shout
at the cats who slouch towards the vacant
lot next door as my father opens the door
and steps out into the cold. He won't

last another winter but he doesn't know
that yet. I wave him back inside to keep
warm at the first fire he's had to build
this season. Bone-coloured smoke rises
straight into the air; the engine turns

over and I back out onto the road. My girl
wants to know why we need to grow old,
as I drive her away from me
towards her first day alone.

Remembering her bad dream, my daughter
wants to let the fish go. This is the same
fish that whispered to her in her sleep,
warned her, "You have seen God, seen him
lead you towards the river, felt the knife
that was meant for me." We tried
to comfort her, took her fishing as if to prove
not all dreams were true; I carried a knife
to clean the fish afterwards even though she cried
to hold it, to show us she could be so careful.

Her father wanted her to bait a hook,
but she flinched and turned from him
because a hook had to hurt, it had to
hurt in the parts of the body raw
sunlight never reaches.

When the fish struck her father lifted it,
gold in the flashing morning, and our daughter
pleaded with him to let the fish go. She said
a silver fish would be luckier, it would glint
in the shallows like a dipped knife:
let the gold carp go, take his bad luck back
to where mysteries remained unexplainable.

We didn't know better; we hurried
the body to higher ground and laid it out
under the sun where it seemed to sigh
as if wishing it could have been silver, luckier.

We didn't know what to do and in that
moment when the gold carp held us wavering
in its eyes, my daughter seized the knife away
and plunged towards the certainty of the river.

MUTE SWANS

All winter you stared into the deep harbour
where, that last summer, our two children
drowned. You wore a red shirt to their service,
though red was never a colour I'd associated,
until then, with mourning. But you had always
refused to mourn or inhabit your body
until you filled it again with enough heroin
to make it safe. Our daughters were buried

in a common grave under a shade tree
chosen for its shallow roots. I believe
we held hands while we picked the grave,
at least allowed our fingertips to touch,
before I walked back alone to serve tea
and the lifeless cakes a grieving neighbour
had provided. The coffin seemed so plain,
whiter than the mute swans our eldest daughter
had painted last spring before your hands
began to shake and the world became
the colour of bruised veins. I try

to remember the immense beauty of pain,
the boat shimmering red like the rush
of blood you sucked up every hour
into a syringe. The children were too far
out, too young to know anything
about drowning, and you so unable to lift
your arms to save them. We buried them

wearing identical dresses even though
in life I'd never dressed them in anything
the same. I let someone else choose,
a specialist who said white was the most
innocuous colour, the one least likely

to incite strong emotion. My friends
thought I had no feelings because I couldn't
weep, not even when the red boat
was hauled to the surface of the green water
with its limp cargo, and those small
bodies full of choked water lay wrung out
on the beach. I gave up feeling, what use

would it have been to feel? At night
when you nodded off by the window
I took turns in their twin beds, turning down
the covers as if they still might move
over and make room for me. On the wall
above the beds, the unfinished watercolour;
I remember our eldest daughter
making her young sister pose, a sheet
draped over her teetering body, her white
wings closed. After the death

it was your stillness I could not bear,
the way you sat waiting,
as if you expected two mute swans to alight
upon our world, our life, and give us
light in darkness. Sorrow is nothing.
Small things keep us safe.

THE WAY WE WATCH FOR HER

We put her body into the ground. There,
I've said it, the words, finally.
It's taken me a lifetime to say
we put her body in the ground
and the ground wept. We believed
we found forgiveness in the earth's
grief, a kind of effortless despair in the shock
of wet dirt we dug through before striking
those tumbling roots. You see, we couldn't
bury her where anyone would come
across her. There's no marker, nothing to say
her trusting naked body lies in peace. Only
a mound just out of reach under the nettles
and wild peppermint. We have good reasons
for keeping her grave untouched, and those
reasons will go to our own graves

with us. We put her body into the ground
squeezing her inside the weightless coffin
the way she squeezed herself into the shining
blue leotards she lived in: even the earth squealed
when she kicked and did the splits.

She was so alive, exquisitely unaware of her own
existence as she cartwheeled across the heavens,
somersaulting into the star-struck universe.
How small death seemed in her spinning sky.
How true the sound of our weeping.

a ten-year-old boy going to the park
armed with his father's rifle.
It's dark, it's the dead of summer
and he's come to pick off a few ducks,
the kind used to being kept
who won't be missed by anyone. The boy
takes his little sister with him.

His father has shown him how
to use the gun. "Imagine," the father says,
"there's a killer in front of you.
This gun is all you have." The boy
has sighted the ducks from his bedroom
window. All week he's been waiting
and when the right moment comes

he takes his little sister
to be his decoy. She loves ducks
though he's forgotten she's not old enough
to know you have to sneak up on them.

He wants his first shot to be true
like the kisses of his mother who thinks
her children are already safely sleeping.
He has deceived her before and she might
forgive him again this time
if he's resourceful. He raises his father's
sniper rifle towards the spectre of his
little sister running. She goes flying
towards the birds, crying
"Bang!" to the killer inside him.

Sailing south up the north coast
of Labrador, tired of photographing whales,
icebergs — *All nature is but art unknown*
to thee — tired of my imagining self, I go
back to my cabin and read — *All chance,*
direction, which thou canst not see. One
poem sticks: a boy, Eddie, naked under a tree,
tiny penis bleeding from someone's switch,
the same person who has taken photographs
and left the yellow film boxes littered
around the boy's feet. The poem is entitled

"A Violation." Over lunch I discuss
mind-body unity with two Buddhists
from Winnipeg, how each juncture of the healing
journey presents us with a choice, a turning
point — whether to split off
from our experiences or make what has happened
part of our Becoming. I'm struggling

with this, back on deck trying to photograph
a whale breaching, but I'm never quick
enough. I return to my quarters, defeated
by nature and technology. And unable to forget
the violation of Eddie Trainor. It reminds me
of the beating my own brother took: barely six
my father expected him to act

like a man. The bully, an older boy,
straddled my brother and punched him until
his knuckles were raw and my brother's face
a blur of crushed flesh and gracelessness.
Then my father berated him for being weak,
the loser. I believe my brother

split off from himself that day -
And spite of pride, in erring
reason's spite — it was a turning
point in the process of his Becoming
insane. My women friends joke about men being
so insane they won't ever stop
to ask for directions, they always have to
prove themselves and can't get it up any longer
even if you tell them you've got all night.

One truth is clear: whatever is, is right.
Then I remember my two boys as I was
going out the door, my frail sons becoming
fierce, always fighting in those days
over which would be the first one
to kiss his mother goodnight.

WHEN THE WORLD IS NOT OUR HOME

Once we returned to my father's house,
the house he had lived in as a child.
He said he found it unchanged, yet
when I looked at his face I felt
it must have changed. He died just the same,
as if he had been caught scheming

to live forever. That day we walked back
into the breathing fields, the same fields
his own father had planted. And when he stooped
to strip an ear of corn from its cornsilk sheaf
I remember how I blushed, afraid
he would be accused of stealing. I was
much younger then, and always afraid

of losing him. That day, too, we went to see
the family graves. The new owners said
they didn't mind if we stayed all day.
The graves looked abandoned and I wanted
to plant something that would grow there
forever, wild things to rise out of our graves
like late-blooming stars. My father had brought

tea, which we drank on my grandmother's
fallen headstone. He said she was fey
in the old days, and told people's fortunes
under the giant medlar. I wanted to be

her way, and studied the leaves on the bottom
of my tea cup until my father took the empty
cup away. I saw him, breathless, going

into the ground that day. Unable to bear
the way his face accused, I was changed
by loss, also. But looking back
over that day, I miss more now.

ELEGY

It happened in a house I love;
my mother came to me carrying a cradle
with a child's body in it. I watched
how she kissed it and caressed it
then placed the cradle under the clock
that stopped ticking years ago
when I first stopped being
her daughter. I learned to tell time
by my father's lonely silences as he sat
hating the world we lived in.

In the house I loved I learned to hate, also,
the wind all around, the smell of candles
burning. I remember, too, the granite slabs
my father hauled home and laid out
for our new summer patio. They were like
ancient gravestones and I was afraid
to cross over them into the shade,

but what panicked me more was having to sit
in that shade with my father, drawing up plans
for the afterlife. So I went into my own
world, conjuring spirits. My mother
said nothing when the ghosts choked
her hardy annuals, stunted her gentle
perennials. She poured tea for my father
who sat under the dying willow
as it rubbed against the roof and made
our house dangerous to live in.

When my daughter was born in the same house,
years later, her eyes were already ancient.
Time began again and I felt less lonely,
as if I could live in the world from then on
and know what I might expect from it.

Now my mother lights a candle
and the wind carries the light away.
The wind hauls an empty cradle away.

THERE WAS NO GARDEN HERE

when we arrived, only my father's house
in a stony pasture, and a crucifix
nailed to a stunted medlar

to hex the snakes, hundreds of them,
who slipped their way out of the dark earth
to bathe under the shedding sun; I was the kind
of kid who could whup a snake from here
to kingdom come: that was my father's
expression, from here to kingdom come.

When you've had your father's blood
on your face, how can you write about it?
When you walk around in the hat
he shot his head off in, what can you write?

I loved his brown eyes, his voice,
the scent of his pipe tobacco
like wildflower honey mixed with wind.
I imagined the smell of the honeysuckle
he promised to plant each fall
as if anything could take hold in that place
and grow. The night he left he told me
next year I will plant my best garden ever.
And I knew, like all the other mysteries
of his life, it would exclude me. I can still see

the way he pulled the brim of that hat down
over his eyes. And I still hear those snakes
in the black hold of this earth, plotting
their own garden where they could crawl from here
to kingdom come, trying to understand
what it took to be a man.

FAMILY PLOT

We're at my father's grave
planting flowers that won't last
the season. My daughter, aged three,
says if we dig far enough and move
all the earth he might come up again
before summer.

I watch as she picks up a handful
of dirt. For her this is an ordinary
experience. *Come on, I'll show you*
she says when I stop, kneeling there
over a hole in the ground, not wanting
to go deeper than we already have, afraid
to drive the shovel home.

FORCING THE NARCISSUS

I show him what he doesn't want
to see — love is a blind man
playing dice in a blizzard.

He swears these bright flowers
like words when cut will sing or bleed;
I believe he is only grieving
or that grief has a lot to do with it.
Blindness or too much brightness can be
the same thing. He says he wants to see the world
but lacks the simple means of getting there.

I tell him what he doesn't want
to hear — how I woke to find my father
forcing the tears that hung on my eyelashes
like wet gravel, how I felt the wind through
my paper white door. How can I tell him life is less

than he imagines it to be, at the same time more
tangible than anything we know? It is
hard to believe plump bulbs sucked dry
as an old man's testicles will ever sing
or amount to very much. I carry them in
out of the storm to the calm centre
of my father's room where, I'm told,
anything might bloom, it's no sin
to be surprised. In us grows the strange
and the wild barely covered by skin
yet I think how much thinner
is the membrane between myself and the world.

MY FATHER CAME BACK FOR THE FURNITURE

and now he's in the bathtub
where my mother is trying to drown him.
She holds him down by the ankles
while he does a back-stroke rapidly.

In real life he was good
at the breast-stroke. Something is wrong
and my father has an erection
for the first time since 1956,
the year I was conceived if I am
to believe in anything.

I'm embarrassed by what I see.
Later when, without dignity, he's floating
with my sister's bath-toys beached on him
I think, "He has lived." That's all,
there are no other words for it,
nothing to say how degrading death is,
and all the more so for its pettiness.

My mother remains calm and picks up
her knitting. She's making a pair of sleepers
for the baby she'll never bear.

My sister puts her feet on the coffee table
and weeps. I go out the back door and squat
beside a garbage can to piss. When the stray
dog stops to sniff I kick him until he's sick.
I'm so heartless it would take a stone
to break me, my mother says. She doesn't
drop a stitch. Blesses our home.

The night it snowed a man set fire
to his dog near the road. Chained him
to a stake by a pile of burning timber,
a blind dog who would not have believed
such brightness possible.

The villagers came to watch, to warm
themselves at the bonfire. One who was known
to have a way with animals talked about
the cruelty of having to keep a dog tied up.

Beyond the road a woman lay naked
in the first snow. They had tied her legs
open under the crude shelter of the spruce
where they took turns fucking her with the
femur of a pig. But when she wouldn't
shut her eyes as her baby buckled and kicked

they cut out her eyes and buried them deep
inside her. Then the one who had never had
a fighting woman fucked her hard in the black
holes of her face before wiping himself
in her red hair and reeling back to the road
where the heat was beginning to enter
the dog's bones and the man who was known
to have a way with animals started
kicking the fire out. A waning moon

like a breast that lays itself
bare against a child's face, rose
over the snow, and the spaces between stars
grew brighter. The child does not know
almost everything we call art is

the spiritualization of cruelty. She sees
only through the eyes of a naked woman
painting the stars out in the lonely
new silence of her future, as if all
the brilliance she had been reaching for
was in blindness. ·

THE GIFT

In the beginning when your heart wants
to sing "Wild Thing," she turns up
the chamber music and from that point
you won't sleep. She shoots you
full of heroin, Southern Comfort,
her boyfriend's marigold-smelling prick.

When your nerves are half-formed
she takes you shopping for the weapons
you will need to survive with. You play
baby roulette, spinning cartridges faster
than bone cells replace cartilage. You don't
need a whole brain to know the word for hate
in all languages. You understand love
is something that needs to be cut off
like the umbilicus, though there's no knife
long enough to sever your bodies for good.

Before your eyes have opened you know
your childhood belongs to someone else,
a connection who crosses the placenta
and makes your heartbeat wilder than ever.
Heart forming four chambers, vocal cords
complete. You try crying out against
the requiems your mother makes you
listen to, but it's too late now
she has decided to keep you and you feel

her reaching to stitch it up, the sad
equipment of womanhood. You want to console
her, forgive her, for this is her first
experience, and no one has taught her how
to sew. Her bloody fingers poke around
for you, they could hurt you

but before your lips have learned to say
leave me alone you have remembered
you can sing. You sing "Happy Birthday"
until she begins to push. Singing
won't help later when she tries to flush
your crushed head down a public toilet
but it helps you now, moments before
your head is engaged, held still and quiet
in the basin of your mother's bones. Singing

seems to be a kind of salvation. You know
every song about Hell and what to expect
when you get there. Now you're howling your way
down the birth canal, past empty gin bottles
and used syringes. After nine months of happiness
you're learning withdrawal, what it's like to be
fully human, how your mother only gives you all
she's got to give.

POISON

When I was old enough I dug
the eyes from my mother's china doll
and buried them on a beach.
No one could reach me with small
talk of sadness after that: my tears
became the property of Mother-May-I
who always answered, "No-you-may-not".

When I was mad enough I tore the doll's
real hair out by the roots until
my own skull looked like a cool zero with two
holes, a nose and a mouth. No one spoke
of choice as I sat cramped in the back
of the Buick with my mother sighing
how she'd looked at life from both sides
of the same two bits, and my father
threatening to drive the car off
the biggest bluff if she didn't quit.

On the last birthday my mother gave me
a bottomless cup. I felt the first tears strike
my face, gather in the dim mouths
of my eyes as she sat blaming me for her
guttering light. I was her poison
she said, the potion she could count on
when it came to sacrificing love. But by then
I thought only of returning it, unable
to bear the debt of it, this gift
she called my life.

PRAISE

They had gathered in a field, the wild
woman they called witch strapped to a fence-post,
stripped but for her snow-boots of rabbit
and a lemon-coloured scarf. They lit a fire
and watched her burn as their children
poked the meat off her body with sticks.

The men called to me, to warm myself
at her fire; one placed his ox-hide
overcoat on my shoulders, his gloves
of heavy seal-skin on my hands. My mother's
eyes told me to be grateful, I had youth,
I had it all. She must have believed I even had
her man, who slipped his hands inside the overcoat
and caressed me as if he had been aroused
by her pain, and the fire nourished him.

Years later I could see my mother's eyes every time
I took a wedge of lemon between my teeth and sucked
the bitterness dry. I felt her scarf tugging at me
as her voice carried high into the star-pitched sky.
The old man who had once been her young lover
said he'd always believed a warm woman was god

as he'd entered me that night. Even where I burned
he still felt the desire to praise her.

there lay a goat. I sat in the sun
with an old man who sold replicas
of the crucifix, and flowers he laid out
on a torn gravecloth, and oranges.

Children carried sacks of offal
out of the grove, and a sorcerer wrapped
a double rainbow in his rags. I hacked
blood into the beggar's cup as he passed,
a chipped cup with two black teeth at the bottom.

The beggar cried, *the dead have risen!*
The dead have risen! and two guinea-fowl
who had escaped from the market
messed themselves in front of the memorial.
Secretly I was glad. Secretly I had been waiting
for something like this to happen.

Both were dazed, both were bleeding as they
teetered in the shade of the memorial where
the goat was lying. One tried to peck out
the goat's closed eye. The goat didn't move
and I thought *these are our times.*

Later in a room, both of us wanting
everything to be over, I dragged my tongue,
leaving a blood-trail from your legs and belly,
to your mouth.

The Long Way Home

I rode through Paris once.
I was twenty-seven and I'd been
told all taxi-drivers were
untrustworthy, they'd take you
the long way home.

I did not know I was living my life then
for what I have become.

My driver got lost.
At least he said we were lost.
I didn't know the city
so I had to take his word for it.
We drove all night.

I had wanted to be a woman
who could make any man
remember how good it always was
how sweet and sad and good

but I'm only what I am

and I don't remember how the night
ended, or if I caught the
morning train
or if the man awaiting me
in Marseilles was sick with worry
when he met the morning train,
and how the children, if there were
children, kissed me in the rain.

It was the last time I got lost.
I remember how he looked at me
on those dark wide streets
so that I almost stopped doubting him

and later, in the narrow bed
how eager I was to prove I'd always
trusted him, when he said

show me, show me what a man is for

and I did.

DEPRESSION IN DEBRECEN
(Budapest Spring Festival, Hungary, 1993)

Leaving Budapest we pass rows of bruise-coloured
apartment blocks the communists left behind
and a cemetery full of half-dug graves, good
reasons, our interpreter says, to write poetry
about beauty also. The graves stare back
at us as a black train crosses our tracks,
grey faces against the windows blurred
like brushstrokes x-ing out the past.

When I was a child I collected stamps. I had
diamonds immortalizing dead poets, and triangles
with histories of love and heartbreak
that took up three or more spaces in the pages
allocated to Magyar Posta. I don't know
what became of my life, or my desire
to open to those pages and feel the tender
blurring world fall into focus for something
longer than a moment.

In my pocket I turn our room-key in my hand,
so heavy in the new morning it almost feels
weightless. Last night at the hotel, drunk
on Bulls' Blood after a gypsy offered you sex
with a twist in the No Problem Drink Bar,
we fought and you threw my half-packed suitcase
after me as I tried to get away. It hit
the side of my head where memories are locked
and I went back through my life to a dimly lit
room, and my father with his belt the colour
of dark chocolate standing over me, bringing
the world down onto my head.

Our interpreter points to the slaughterhouse
where she once worked and fell in love
with an adulterer. Every day they went home
with blood on their hands, until he confessed.
She is frail and the bones beneath her
sunken face stick out like bones unearthed,
exposed to wind and rain, then buried again.
In Debrecen we drink rare brandy with local writers
and communicate through the only words we have
in common: *man, conflict, depressio, migraine.*

Attila, the poet, asks if I have a migraine
because I keep touching the hurt place
on the side of my head — "Beauty is only
skin deep," our fathers said, caressing the bruises
as if they, too, were blessings bestowed
upon us, blessings we were told to keep counting
every day and so we did. I counted the days
until my father went away for good, then stood
at his grave weeping half in love, half out
of rage. Feeling the raised flesh under

my fingers today, I think — this is my way
of keeping in touch with you, far away
to the south, as if hurt were an horizon
you could ever cross over. "*Mee-graine,*"
says Attila. "*Man. Conflict. Depressio.*"

On the drive back to Budapest I rest
my forehead against the tinted window and watch
black rain beading in my reflection. Years ago
when first in love I would have compared
the streaking rain to tears, though I know better
now. Hungover at the hotel you will be dressing

for dinner in the suit you wore to our wedding
seven years ago, but I won't know what to expect
after so many years when I turn the key in the lock,
as if coming home again could ever be that simple.

Strange to be travelling back through
darkness, too, desiring everything I am
afraid of. Stranger still to centre longing
in the father of a child you will never be
sure of, one who looks back at you through a history
of love and heartbreak and who, without touching,
takes the weighted room-key from your hand.

"HERE IT COMES — GRIEF'S BEAUTIFUL BLOW-JOB"
— William Matthews

Last night for the first time
you told me you loved me less.
I put on a child's dress, pinned
a half-moon to my breast and walked
uptown. The streetlamps kept on
whispering of you as I waited
for one who would love me anyway.

How little it takes to mend, how little
to break. The first man who gave me a ride
had a valentine the colour of blood
under his shirt. He took me for a drive
down the wrong side of the road playing
"Here Comes the Night" so loud I didn't
even hear the real night come crashing
in on me the way it did. Dress of gauze
over my right eye, two fist-shaped moons
under my left. He left me for dead
but it didn't even hurt -

not the way it hurt to be
loved less.

Motif of passion-flowers at the Hoo-Doo Motel,
the kitchen comes fully equipped, the bed
has Magic Fingers. Everything but my heart comes

equipped. The philosopher in the bomber jacket
who says, "'No means bondage, bitch',"
he's equipped. He's a realist. He had a real
whip. He gave me everything except a rag
to wipe the blood up with. He made me strip

then took his realistic jiggler out
and told me there was no one cause
for any human act of degradation.
I'd thought no one could touch me
when it came to self-abuse until he had me
licking my own blood off two cheap passion
flowers on the white lino

but nothing could have prepared me
for this, to be loved less.

When I was a child my father butchered
my first pet, a wild rabbit I'd tamed
and fed until she grew big enough to eat.
Then he killed her with his long hands
and dressed her and made me eat; every day
of my life he forced me to keep eating
until there was nothing left. It was a lesson
in sufficiency, he said.

But when you told me you loved me less,
I didn't know how to cure it.
The bed became smaller than cruelty
with just enough room for the two of us
and the night came over me
like a backhand over the mouth
like my father with steak blood
in the corner of his mouth
holding up a photograph of his
shy, wild daughter.

I wanted to give reasons why I tried to love you
more each day, but it all sounded
so ordinary, like taking a piece of bread
and cutting it. Even this simple act
brings a knife into play

so the moon packs her bags and moves
away. Not me, I'm here for the duration.
Grief's never had it so good.

everything is over between us.
To our late visitor you whisper,
"but she must never know."

You kiss the dice for luck, toss them high
and your luck changes. Deep inside the house
our small daughters are sleeping
in an emptiness they cannot yet put a name to.
As a child I wanted to die, because -
I believed then — nothing could be
more frightening than living.

In the next room I hear you laughing.
You embrace our friend, who one day
will be able to tell me she had never been
held so hungrily, then hug our daughters
and tuck them in to bed. I can feel your arms,
the way the muscles flex like soapstone clouds,
the ancient way they stretched out to me
the first time, earnest as beauty.

I remember, too, how I loved your skin,
tattoo of a spicy wind blowing its
red hot cinnamon heart out to meet my lips
and stick there like an unrepentant kiss.
And I loved your eyes, the pain in them
gentle as the scent of rain in a lemon grove

but you must never know how much
I will always be in love with you.
I who have been so capable of leaving, stay
awake until dawn, just long enough
to call it mourning.

As if It Wasn't

enough to leave me, you've come back.
I've been down at the river
gathering gravel and mud into my arms
and I saw the whole world passing me by,
and it didn't mean much.

You take me in your own arms
and try to comfort me.
You think a kiss, a caress,
can mend anything.
Listen, I've lived too long,
I'm lucky, look at my palms.

I'm a luxury and you know it.
You'd trade all the women
with their wet lips and their words,
you'd trade the feel of their
uncomplicated bodies

for a share of my loneliness,
because I own it.

You can't bear what I know.
And as if it isn't enough
you try to take me
as if I were whole and ordinary

but you don't like it after all,
the distance in me.

I suppose you'll leave.
I'm getting used to it
and it doesn't mean much.

I'm familiar with the easy way
it goes badly from the beginning
when the heart first closes itself to hope
like a tired woman stooping
to scoop the river up.

This Is the Day

I have nothing under my skirt
but a whole lot of lessons I never learned
properly. The man labouring on the road
senses that, and waves a fingerless hand
hoping for a quick throw over the lunch hour.

Your life isn't your own any more
when a man like that can bruise his eyes
on emptiness, and leave you wanting.
In a huff I move from the stoop

into the house where my friends have laid
a feast around my body. It's been dying
for days and they've dusted it -
she would have wanted it that way -
with cake flour to make it look ghostly.

I don't want it, who would want anything
like it? I fume around the place for awhile
but there is no outlet now, there never was.
It seems a shame to have loved a man so long
who was the wrong man

but suddenly there comes a day when I can move
through a room without you. And this
is the day.

MEETING YOU AGAIN

I don't know which fear rose in me
as we walked the frozen road through
Sudden Valley back to the hotel where we'd met
after a nine-month separation, to make
love all the long night, the same night
John Lennon died in New York.

I remember wearing your shoulder holster
to the door when room service came
with wild salmon from the Similkameen
and hot chocolate we spiked with *aguardiente*
you'd smuggled in your luggage from Colombia.
I wore, too, an antique Tibetan vest,
and my breasts swung free as bells,
and when I tipped the ancient waiter
he said, "Have a pleasant evening, folks,"
and I could see we had given him pleasure.

It could have been the fear of losing you
to Elizabeth, a hunchback from Bogotá
whose scarlet fingernail you carried
like a love charm close to your heart
in a pocket of your stone-coloured overcoat.
It was lucky I knew, to touch a hunchback's
hump, to take on some of that
loneliness, but I'd never be a match

for Elizabeth who wrote poetry to you
in *Spanish*, poetry you told me
was untranslatable. My love, the words
I love you are words I'd recognize
in any language, no matter how foreign.
Or it could have been the fear of losing

myself in the wholeness of your body,
as, back then, I believed it was.

These days my body is filled with a kind
of singing; I ask you not to think of pain
when you come to listen to me. Think
instead of the white air, the pure light
we breathed together on that distant morning
in Sudden Valley, how you stopped me
from speaking about the future back then,
as if any kind of love could fail.

RECEIVING END OF LOVE

You've been told you have a nose that can
sniff out the bad in any man, a heart
vacant as twin beds at the Paradise Motel.
You've been rode hard and put away wet
so many times now, at first

you feel useless, being on the receiving
end of love. At first there's nothing left
but the desire to make the best of it;
on the back lot in a strip of light
you join your names in blood.
But when his hand slips and he unloads
the machine-gun in your head,
you're forever his.

At first you feel an awful lot
is happening, and then you get
desperate, not knowing if it's happiness,
until one night on a trick
bed he ties your wrists to the posts
and slips a coin between your lips. You flip
it twice on your tongue, sucking
this big spender into your back pocket right
where you always wanted him

and then you get down, shaking
your hips in memory of a rhythm
you once lived your life to, making it.

Hair Dream

If you dream of finding hairpins
of a rival woman you are being
deceived by your mate or maybe
you are deceiving him and you
don't know it. Either way the dream is
undeniable like a reversible scarf caught
in the spokes of a speeding convertible.
You once knew two sisters who died and had
their bodies laid to rest under a shag
carpet. People stepped on them, the dog
slept on them, but their red hair kept growing
up through the rug. It lay humped
across the rug like old road-kills
while their relatives tried backcombing
the life back into it. This reminds you
of the hospital where families of people
in comas brush and keep brushing, hoping
the comatose can tell. You sing *only*
the comatose until someone tells you
to shut up. She whispers that you should
kill yourself, but he's not worth that
much. You take the hairpins he has
arranged on your pillow and rearrange
them into the shape of an erect penis, bigger
than one he ever dreamed of. Oh, what's this?
he might say, when he comes to bed wearing
a lampshade over his head to keep his
Mohawk from being flattened. Hairpins
you might reply. But you hear the question

in your own voice and think of Osiris
dying without issue, and Isis warming
his body with her hair until his heart
turned over and his penis moved and how she
worked him over all night drawing his essence
out of him, all the time sweating only slightly
at the roots of her dutifully combed hair.

EXCHANGE OF FIRE

When your left arm touched my right
as we both reached for the dessert
menu in the all-night diner, a spark
began smouldering in my sleeve, broke
a hole the size of a heart in the patched
elbow of your jacket.

Dirty white smoke enveloped our bodies
as the conversation turned
to the underground fire we'd all seen
on the news, a fire that had raged up
to consume everything in its path.
The air in the diner stank of charred meat;
under the table I took my husband's right
hand and placed it on my left thigh
where flesh and garter meet.

I wanted only that, until your left knee
grazed my right, and this time
there was an explosion, just as our waiter
lit the Crepes Suzette your wife had ordered
for you. Flames engulfed our table
and we moved to another booth, my husband
and your wife saying *we can't take
you two anywhere* simultaneously.

I had to decide: should I risk
asking for something sweet now, or abstain? -
when you said think of the women on the Titanic
who pushed away from dessert that night
because their skirts were getting tight.
It made me think all right

and then when we were all friends again,
laughing, the whole length of your left leg
rubbed the length of my right and every
light in the joint went out, life stopped
for me, it meant a scandal somewhere in the future.

I tried to focus on the scorched dessert
menu feeling the beginnings of violent
pleasure. I reached for my knee where the hair
had been singed off, where the flesh was
already oozing, and I remember thinking,
I like this. It was the beginning
of loneliness, also.

For when the lights came back on I was
afraid to move from my seat; when we rose
to say goodnight we would be expected
to embrace. We had to: the flesh

of your body down the length of my trembling
body, the thin cloth covering my breasts
covered with flames, the apologies to your wife
for the plastic buttons on your shirt front melting,
your belt buckle welding us together in our heat.

At home I'm still burning when my husband
pours lighter fluid on his hands and feet and sets
himself on fire: only by entering fire can I
put the fire out. This time I might finally
do it. It may be a threat, an end to pain,
or all there is left to make of love.

THIS DAY

The man whose wife is afraid
I have fallen in love with him
asks, *why do I always lie*
whenever I've placed everyone in danger?
He lies naked on their unmade bed
and I place my wedding ring
on the end of his half-erect penis

before slipping it back
onto the tip of my tongue. I do not care
why he lies. This spring I have become
obsessed with danger, my children
in the wild garden flapping
like birds his wife has attracted
to the feeder. I ask him if he will
remember this day but I know already
he has forgotten it, ear cocked to something
beyond, beating back the growth.

THE SEX OF MONEY

You walk into the white field, squat
between rows of frozen cabbages, almost happy
he is gone. You spread the money all around
you on the ground, remembering how warm
it felt when he put it in your hands.

POSSIBILITIES

Purple vetch and wild roses
mark the edge of the clearing
where you in a white robe bend
over a green bowl sinking your face
in rain. Foxgloves and blue
lupine reach for the sky
where the stars are lined up
like targets you could have
picked off blindfolded.

"There are possibilities for me, but
under what stone, beloved, do they lie?"
I heard my mother's cradle song
the first time I undid my dress
for you in the cemetery, and squatted
without panties, in stinging nettles
over my father's grave to show
how far I'd go. The pain excited me
because of the possibilities
because of what could happen
if you once sunk your face
into my white breasts or rubbed
cool mint leaves between my thighs.

Now I know where our possibilities lie
coming back to you this last time
with day breaking. I gather
Queen Anne's Lace for the table
beside your bed, and Mock Orange

white as the morphine you take
every odd hour for pain. In my life
I've made choices, now I've come to you
the whole distance. From our window I see
wild strawberries, like hearts,
swelling amongst mint leaves.

ARCTIC POPPIES

After a week of rough seas the ship docked
at Hopedale. The weather was no good but still
I struggled ashore and climbed to the desecrated
churchyard, determined to take away something
of a memory, to photograph the white Arctic
poppies. Each time I framed a shot, my hands
steady at last, a hunchback on crutches teetered
into sight, as if innocently waiting for the fog
to lift, the rain to let up, the light
to throw open its dingy overcoat and expose
itself to my nakedness. My eye, my whole body
had been saving itself for this, but every time
he humped into view, I thought of you, the best
man I'd ever left, lips tasting of whatever you'd had
to eat: spicy eggplant baba ghanoug, jumbo
shrimp in garlic and Chablis, your mother's
meat pie with a dash of cinnamon
and cloves. When the sun broke

through I'd have those wild flowers posed,
I'd be poised to shoot and then the stooped
shadow would fall as if to say beauty
without imperfection was something to be
ashamed of, as if he could be my flaw.
Crouched beside an abandoned grave
I tried to focus on those white
poppies in light that went on failing,
seeing your perfect body in his
crippled gaze. I could have taken him

back to my cabin aboard the ship, laid
his crutches down, bathed him, bent over
his grateful body and licked the smell
of smoked trout and caribou hide from his
thighs. Perhaps this is what he hoped for,
and then to be called beautiful afterwards.

I took his photograph. He'd wanted that, too
and suddenly I felt blessed, I felt
I'd been taken the way I liked it best: sex
in the head on sacred ground that has been
roughed up a little, a graveyard full
of ghostly poppies choking out the dead.

Razor-Wire, Millhaven Penitentiary

It slices through my heart
the way it surrounds you,
and something the colour of blood
spills out. In so much blackness
the heart leaps, jumps a beat
by the wall, goes over.

You've slashed your hands on the wind,
your eyes on a woman's body,
but nothing, not even the stars going out,
has hurt as much as this.

The heart is a gash
and the sky glitters, but all
that high wire coiled and ready to cut
can't keep tenderness out.

The distance between us
is the thickness of blood. Love
jumps away, jumps
out of us.

In the Small Hours of the Rain

"Sorrow is nourishment forever."
— Carolyn Kizer

I'm leaving again
and Stephen's sad-night eyes
fill the darkness. Behind his eyes
the world's pain becomes
something I am grateful for,
something tried but unpredictable
that darts into the heart and leaves
its ragged truth there.

I've got scars to prove it.
I've never belonged to anyone.
Now his eyes fill that emptiness
with something beyond love
and I can't get enough of it:
like grief, there's never enough.

Coming Home, Summer

Across the bay, lightning. I had wanted
to be small rain on your face, no heavier
than a human tear. When you walk in
out of that storm how easy it would be
to say, touch me. How trusting
you look. How I brush back my hair.

Things That Keep and Do Not Change

Out on the windy gulf, breakers
like bouldery sheets of laundry
tumble and spin towards the horizon
in my sleep. We've been fogbound for three days
and I've learned the difference between bad
ice and good, how to travel in a blizzard
using the wind to set your course.

One night I woke and a white shadow
was trying to get into bed with me.
My tongue went numb and the only words
I could remember came out cold. I used to think
white was no colour at all, only your absence
making itself known, your ghost
doubling back to pull down my stiff
winter underwear from our drooping clothesline -
little thief! When they found you
the foam on the beach after the north wind
blew all night was white and deep.
We've been fogbound for days
and I've learned to set my course on the wind.

1: How Portable My Pain

On New Year's Day my love went away
and left me with nothing
but the poems of Paul Durcan.
There are worse things a man can do
than leave a woman alone
with the poems of Paul Durcan.

I read, and wept, then read some more
and pretty soon I had fallen in love
with the enormously lonely selected
poems of Paul Durcan.

And as I took a train from the west
out of Ballinasloe later that evening
with a pocket full of earth-smelling
potatoes I'd purchased as a gift
for the poet in his lonely Ringsend bedsit,
the signs were all around me: Wrinkles Beauty
Salon, Nutter's Bar & Spirits, Wacker's
Pet Shop, UP IRA — I knew I was on my way

into the centre of the universe
of a poem by Paul Durcan. I could picture
myself tapping at his small door
in the calm centre of the universe,
not knowing what I would have to say
if only he ever answered. I tell you

when I got there I found a note
banged to that door saying sorry for leaving me
stranded, he might be across the road consoling
the jilted neighbour whose lover had run off

with a blonde telephonist from Ulster leaving her
with six highly illegitimate children

or he could be down the street calming
the good woman Mrs. Murphy whose husband practices
self-exposure in front of the television leaving her
with feelings of self-recrimination

or possibly he was up the way placating
the recently widowed beauty whose husband
had torched her wardrobe: by now I had begun
to realize it was by no means a simple thing
to be sucked into the whirlpool at the centre
of the universe of a poem by Paul Durcan.

My head was full of interrogation marks,
I won't deny, and oh, I don't know,
I stood there, my pocket full of those
dark earth-smelling potatoes, which I
considered leaving on his doorstep
in the shape of the ultimate interrogation mark

all the while telling myself there are worse things,
yes, far worse things a man can leave a woman with
than the selected poems of Paul Durcan.

2: Lift Up the Stone, You Will Find Me There

I lost the keys to the car
on the strand at Slyne Head.
I had put the keys in my windbreaker
pocket that had a hole in it
without thinking because I had been
thinking about the poems of Paul Durcan.

I found a round stone with a hole in it
while thinking about the poems of Paul Durcan.
The hole in the stone didn't go
all the way through, not like the hole
in the pocket of my windbreaker did go
all the way through: I lost that lucky

stone, also, and I was a long way from home.
Just then I felt like writing the world's loneliest
poems but Paul Durcan had already written them
and I was travelling with my mother, anyway,
who hates the wind. This is what she says
to me, she says, "I hate the wind." I wanted
to say to her how can you *hate* the wind
but I could tell she had made up her mind
about it already. And that was that.

I lost the keys to the car, the car
to the keys, Registration number DS VF263
and my mother hated the wind. On the strand
at Slyne Head I put the car in my windbreaker
pocket that had a hole in it
without thinking because I had been
thinking about the poems of Paul Durcan.

3: Our Sin Will Find Us Out

In Clifden I lay in bed with Paul Durcan
and his selected poems, in bed wearing nothing
but my white flannelette nightie
with what looks like chicken parts all over it,
thinking of him in his bed wearing nothing
but the women's pyjamas he bought
thinking they were men's pyjamas
at Marks and Spencer's in Dublin.
If I had known his number
I would have telephoned to describe
the scent of cock
and hen grilling, a scent that filled my head
as I read, much out of breath, his selected
poetry. I was unable to detect the source
of that scent, checked under my spare
pillow, searched under the bed. I even
sniffed the pages of his book and then

there we were, standing together on the Old Bog
Road between Murvey and Ballyconneely, me
wearing nothing but my white flannelette nightie
with what looks like chicken parts all over it,
and you in the women's pyjamas you bought thinking
they were men's pyjamas in Dublin.

4: The Light That Puts Out Our Eyes

My mother spent her morning searching
the room for a pair of black
woolen socks she bought yesterday
in Westport. I could have stayed
in bed forever reading the selected poems
of Paul Durcan but my mother's sighing
made me anxious, and I got out of bed, placed
his open book on the table next
to my nerve pill collection
and started to take a breath. It was then
I noticed a few page numbers in his book
had gone missing, and, when I looked further,
the title had disappeared, also. Paul,
what has become of you? Don't leave me alone
on this road to Sligo with my barefoot
mother weeping for some wool socks
she bought yesterday in Westport while I climbed
into the black hills with nothing but your book
between my breasts and the wind. I prefer that
nakedness to how I am now, driving the grieving
road to Sligo with nothing but a pair
of black socks, inside out, blinding my eyes.

5: We Count Them Happy Who Endure

After the Cliffs of Moher we took the road
inland to have tea and cheese toasties
at Kilfenora. Even though my mother
was tired I read her the poem I had written
to my father, who, when the time came,
wouldn't fit in his coffin. "I suppose
it's lovely," she told me "and probably true.
But I don't understand a word of it."

Later, in an Ennistymon guest house
while my mother rested, I found, in the selected
poems of Paul Durcan, a poem where his mother
said she did not comprehend a word of his new
book, the poems he had composed to *his* dead father.

I wanted to read my mother this poem, too,
and say, look Mum, Paul's mother feels the same
as you. But I didn't. Not yet. Instead
I took her back to the black
coast of Doolin and Doonbeg where the water,
black, was the colour of my father's
dying light. Black, black. You, Paul,
of all, might understand that.

6: What Peace We Often Forfeit

Because I feared Aer Lingus
Flight 374 would explode in mid-air
en route from Shannon to London
over the Irish Sea, I took on board
with me the selected poems of Paul Durcan.
That way I would have something to cling
on to, something to clutch that would forever be
a comfort to me, with Mr. Garvey, in the seat
next to me, an explosives expert on his way
to London to deliver a lecture, and my mother
in the aisle seat, set to go off.
When he wasn't defusing bombs, so to speak,
Mr. Garvey said, he spent his time writing
verse, specifically about terrorism
and generally about agricultural practises
in Ireland during the famine,
most of which were bleak. Mr. Garvey knew
too, many of the poems
of Paul Durcan having been privileged
to memorize them during his term at Mullingar
Mental Hospital. As we dipped
over the Irish Sea he said he'd always feared
the resurgence of his insanity, would I let him
wear my copy of the selected poems
of Paul Durcan on his knee, or, better still,
around his neck as a kind of oxygen mask
or a life jacket? This is how I came to part

with my solitary copy of the selected poems
of Paul Durcan. I felt considerably ill
at ease until we landed at London's Heathrow
where Mr. Garvey wanted to know would I
accompany him to dinner and an old film

starring Mickey Rourke in Leicester Square,
the one where he blows up
a schoolbus full of innocent schoolchildren.
Only Mr. Garvey called them *"so-called* innocent
schoolchildren" and for that he was not
allowed to leave the plane, nor, as far as I know,
board any other, not ever. I left him
sitting there, Row 3, Seat B, the poems
of Paul Durcan open on his knee. "Strange bird,"
my mother said, as we boarded our Canadian
flight, the one that would carry us on home
after a brief stop to refuel in Calgary.
When the hot meal was served somewhere
over Reykjavik my mother poked around
in it, and seemed pleased. "I'm glad
this chicken doesn't have a bone," she said.
"I wondered how I was going to cope."

A Friend Writes to Thank Me
for Chinese Willow Used in the Art
of Japanese Flower Arranging

Arranging and imagining, I have taken
my pleasure; mutilating and bending
the green stems, how you cut them for me
where I might bend, also, and allow
my own body to be flayed, the raised flesh
under my fingers today in some ways
like binding feet or boarding up
an infant's head: beauty here,
beauty there. I've known men
go faint with passion over hair
on the legs of a woman, others breathless
over a pierced nipple, a stretched neck.
Who's to say. Thanks again, anyway.

Canadian Roulette

Let's not invent any more weapons.
Let's grope in the fog
wearing coarse wool underwear instead.
Let's be kind to one another
and let's not write any more hate poetry.

Let's pretend we're in love with one another.
You go first.

SUSAN MUSGRAVE has published poetry, fiction, non-fiction, and children's literature. Her most recent titles include: *You're in Canada Now . . . A Memoir of Sorts* (essays, Thistledown Press); *Cargo of Orchids* (novel, Knopf), which became a national bestseller; and, *Obituary of Light: the Sangan River Meditations* (poems, Leaf Press). Musgrave is also an editor, and has lent her writing ability to film and music. Her projects have won numerous awards that are as diverse as the bp Nichol Poetry Chapbook Award and the National Film Board's Kathleen Shannon Award. Musgrave was included in the 2008-2009 Royal BC Museum Free Spirit Project that featured the province's most famous and infamous people. Musgrave divides her time between Vancouver Island and Haida Gwaii/the Queen Charlotte Islands. Susan Musgrave's website: www.susanmusgrave.com